THE QUEEN OF HAPP!NESS

...and other poems that will
pick you up,
dust you off,
and lead you to a happier tomorrow
(even if you don't really like
most poetry)

First Printing: 2020

ISBN <978-1-7348095-0-3>

Mindshift Books
Chino, CA 91708

For more information on Tina Ann, Queen of Happiness,

http://www.thequeenofhappiness.com

tinaann@thequeenofhappiness.com

or to see quantity and other special discounts go to

http://www.thequeenofhappiness.com

Dedication

To the Wild Bunch, the Fab 5,
the hearts of my heart, the arrows
to my bow, the inspirations for all
goodness in my life -- my children:
Nicholas, Amanda, Benjamin, Amelia
and Hannah
(and all extended family ensuing)

These poems were born of
my dream of a better world
for each of you.

"For life goes not backward nor tarries with yesterday.
You are the bows from which your children as living arrows are
sent forth."
– Khalil Gibran

Table of Contents

Introduction

Since I love thinking, reading and studying about happiness in its many forms, the poems offered here are part of my journey to understand happiness and all its implications in our lives.

Written over a span of more than 20 years, some were written for specific people, events or purposes, some as a compulsion, some as self-motivation.

Sometimes, while writing or planning a new poem, I simply listen... to the ages... to the whispers... to the messages riding on the aether. Many times, I am simply translating those images and feelings and somehow, it always seems, those translations come out expressed in rhyme!

The offerings cover, of course, happiness, but also hard times, our connection with the heavens and the grace all around us.

My hope is that these poems get you thinking about your own happiness as well as all that you have overcome, the blessings you have been given from the heavens above and the family and friends around you.

May you reach for this book time and again and may the messages it contains continue to speak to you.

If you like what you read, I would love if you would leave me a review!

~Tina Ann, The Queen of Happiness

Forward

To be asked to write the foreward for a friend is an honor. To be tasked to write one for a writer is, well, intimidating at best, especially for me. As a Sound Healer, literally, words are not my forte. I use sound and vibration as a way to improve my client's physical, mental, emotional health. uplift them spiritually and help raise their vibration. Those same benefits can be achieved through Tina Ann's lyrical sounds in the form of poetry. The irony, or to be more exact, poetic justice, is not lost on me. Having been intimately involved with each other's lives going on 25 years, through the milestones, weddings, births, divorces, sacred reunions, the calling becomes an honor.

Tina Ann and I had an instant connection, have an amazing ability to brainstorm, our creative juices flowing through the laughter, finding joy and conquering any obstacle, mostly because, well, she has always been The Queen of Happiness. With Tina Ann, life is a series of building fairy houses, pumpkin carving, beach BBQs, summer pool parties, 4th of July parties, holiday boat parades, 40th 50th 60th celebrations. Blessed to have shared many Thanksgivings and Christmases together watching her fabulous five children grow and prosper, more beautiful every day, and now, sorry have lost count, incredible grandchildren, we are partners, theater buddies, confidants, and have even been roommates.

After being president of our homeowner's association for 10 years, I called upon Tina Ann to replace me, and she took on the task with gusto, shaping the mission fun. During her tenure, we created cutest pet contests, holiday decorating contests, and produced outstanding concerts in the park.

Have you recognized the common thread here? Yes, it's fun, it's laughter, it's happiness! After all, we are talking about The Queen of Happiness!

To help before her divorce, she came for a weekend and stayed for 8 months... and we came through it all, better friends, knowing we can always count on each other

Long ago, Tina Ann shared her poetry writing talents with me. I was in awe! In my alternate life, I've been a computer consultant and webmaster since 1981. The brainstorming duo went to work... her writing more mind stimulating poetry... me creating her website, PersonalVerses.com. Although in serious need of updating, created so long ago, it still shows her diverse body of work. Tina Ann's custom poem that she wrote for my parent's 50th wedding anniversary was such a hit it was a no brainer to ask her to write a poem for my Dad's 80th birthday celebration. Both poems are unique, works of art that will be in family memories forever.

After inviting her to one of my sound healing events, Tina Ann immediately felt the immense effects of my gongs, Tibetan singing bowls, gemstone crystal bowls, and other highly healing, vibrational instruments. She wanted to be a part, be there every time, and we figured out I could use her help. She calls herself my Roadie... I lovingly call her my Sound Healing Angel and am blessed with her beautiful energy and presence, and eternally grateful for her colossal help.

So, Tina Ann and I have some history... all just wonderful... and in hindsight... there are no mistakes... who better to pen a foreward for this absurdly talented poet than someone who may remember these events and details, perhaps better than she does. I can hear her now saying... 'oh, I forgot about that.' I'm reminded how honored I was to help her produce and introduce her at her first original poetry reading many years ago because I believe in her and know first-hand and very well of her talents. Oh, did I mention she won 1st place at the Orange County Fair for her unique, repurposed jewelry boot in the miscellaneous craft category. We all were tickled to bequeath our 'what do we do with' priceless (to us), maybe broken old jewelry, and in turn, feel part of her win. That's what Tina conceives. Always creative, always inclusive, with the ability to turn trash into treasures.

Each one of Tina Ann's poems can stand on their own, each one rich in vast stories and layers of lavish content and emotion. That this collection of poems is together for the first time in her first book is a genuine work of art. The talents of this beautiful soul, that I get to call my friend, are boundless and enthusiastic. Venturing into stand-up comedy, she faces her fears head on, makes it a festival... then what does she do with the experience? Writes a poem, of course. Tina Ann is a natural storyteller, a delightfully fun person, extraordinarily bright and intelligent, and genuinely emanates happiness. I'm honored to be included in any part of her journey.

'Why did you do this all for me?' he asked. 'I don't deserve it. I've never done anything for you.' 'You have been my friend.' replied Charlotte. 'That in itself is a tremendous thing.' – E.B. White, Charlotte's Web

Arjan ♥
sacredSoundJourney.com
aka Lin Marelic
computerTherapist.net

HAPPINESS

Section 1: Happiness

Years ago, I found myself entrenched in an unexplainable bout of the blues. It emerged out of nowhere and resulted in days on end of unnamed sadness and not having the motivation or the (normally unlimited) energy to do anything.

One day, I spoke about it with a good friend. "I think I'm depressed!" I told her. My friend was a little shocked, too, and responded by saying, "No, no, you can't be depressed. You are the queen of happiness!" We both laughed and I did not give it much more thought.

The next day, while looking for the least horrible thing to watch on TV, I heard what seemed like a voice whispering in my ear—a regal voice of exceeding kindness but unquestioning authority which said, "The Queen of Happiness would not behave so dismally."

I heard her so clearly! Oh, my, she even had an English accent and sounded strangely like the Queen of England.

"The Queen of Happiness would get up and get moving," she continued. "She is perfectly aware the people are depending on her."

I gasped. She was relentless! She knew!

And so, she visited me again and again over the next many days, offering practical advice, leading me back each time to gratitude for the blessings already in my life, helping me see the irony in grudges I was holding on to, in spite of the forgiveness I had been shown.

Slowly my perspective shifted from one of want to one of gratefulness, from focus on myself to a focus on others. She guided me toward joy and peace.

This inner Queen of Happiness nudged me into beginning a journey that has brought me to where I am today—my happiest self, my most confident, content and creative self. It fuels the fire behind the burning desire to write about the choices that we face each day.

Today, my alter-ego the Queen of Happiness helps me to share the joys of life. She reminds me to live in the moment, to find the good, to be grateful, to breathe deeply, to smile, to let go of all expectations, and finally—and most importantly—to forgive, everyone, everything, including myself.

In that light, I offer these first poems.
May they bring *you* Happiness!

Enjoy!

~Tina Ann aka The Queen of Happiness

THE QUEEN OF HAPPINESS

In times that you are feeling down
Or giving into stress,
Just have a conversation with
The Queen of Happiness
She knows we have the tendency
To only see and find
All the "Rotten Things in Denmark" that have
Occupied our mind

And that, despite all of our efforts to
Maintain a certain tone,
There are, sometimes, it seems, that we are
Negatively prone
Finding all our thoughts and moods
Under a funky cloud
Allowing all those voices in our heads
To talk aloud
If you pay the Queen a visit
She will sit you firmly down,
And remind you what it takes to pull
A smile from a frown
'Cause sometimes we forget that all of
Joy is ours to claim
If we leave it on the table,
We have just ourselves to blame

The Queen rules with an iron fist
And won't tolerate descent
Into the fog of hopelessness
Or baggage of lament
She knows when you indulge yourself
And sit around and mope,
"There simply is no chance," we whine,
"To turn despair to hope."

She doesn't give the answers
or wave a magic wand,
She simply asks the questions
and then asks you to respond
Since the answers to her questions
Can all be found inside,
Just waiting to be brought to light,
No more to be denied

She kicks the process off
With this pleasing little quest,
Of listing all you're grateful for
And all the ways you're blessed
She asks you to remember
The forgiveness you've been shown,
Then next she has you do the count
Of all the ways you've grown

It's not that problems disappear
Or no longer have a place.
She just reminds us happiness depends
On what we will embrace,
That what we focus on and hold
Determines what we feel,
And good or bad or right or wrong,
It's what will be made real

The Queen reminds us anytime
We happen to forget
That the power to be happy is
As easy as it gets
She brings it all into the fore,
That it's all up to me
Since "Most folks are about as happy as they
Make up their minds to be."

Note: "most folks are about as happy as they make up their minds to be? Abraham Lincoln (?)

https://quoteinvestigator.com/2012/10/20/happy-minds/

SMILE, SMILE, SMILE

When you feel down or out of sorts
And all you have are loud retorts,
Tired of fighting and acting tough
You've been this way for long enough
Hoping that a better way
Will turn around a hard, dark day

So make your bad mood disappear
By taking charge and making cheer
Instead of picking fights, begin
Inviting all the world to grin
Throughout the day, you'll soon agree
That when you greet each one you'll see
That folks are waiting for that invite
They want to smile at you despite
Their fear of the expected hurtful burn
If their smile is not returned

But when you're first to flash your pearly whites
You'll be amazed at what ignites
And when you start to beam unchecked
You'll get back more than you project!
The cheer you gave and got combined
To create just what you searched to find
You had the secret all the while
Hold up your head and
Smile! Smile! Smile!

A KINDNESS DEFICIT

There's a kindness deficit all around,
Examples in our lives abound
Entitled to never feel annoyed,
Sarcastic tactics oft employed
To broadcast to the world at large,
We feel so much better when we discharge

But it could have gone another way
If we chose different words that say
That we are here to lift you up
Inspire the soul and fill the cup
When all it takes to make their day
Is one quick smile and a kind way

And though we travel all alone
Though some of us are far from home
Surrounding us in all we do
Are strangers who are travelling, too

Sure, we could brush past the surrounding crowd
Declare *our* needs, both long and loud
Get ahead, no matter what the cost
Win the prize, no matter how much is lost
Forging ahead until we're prone
Arriving at the finish line ahead – and alone

So pick your path each and every day
You get to choose it in every way
In every hug, in every word
In *every* thought that's felt and heard
We bring the light or put it out
That's what this trip is all about

Your phone can never like you back
Computers just don't cut you slack
Like the real live people around you do
And they're the ones who'll bring you soup

So, be the one who brings the fight
OR be the one who brings the light
Be the smile that can be counted on
Be grateful for all you've had and done

Kind in every word and deed
Be the one to take the lead
To fill the kindness deficit
Each day and every chance you get
There's more of us than you can know
Our Super Power is to let it show!

Together we'll change a whole world view
Let's begin, today, with me and you!

HAPPINESS

Not a place you're looking for,

Nor ever will you arrive

For it's about the way you look

At every moment you're alive

Right this moment, here and now,

Are you basking in delight?

Or perhaps enjoyment best describes

This moment's burst of light

And sometimes just acceptance

Is all that we can do

Since we know that life is blessed

Every day and through and through

As long as we are focused

On whatever is at hand

You'll find whate'er you're looking for,

Each moment, your command

JUST BEGIN

The plan is set, the path is clear
To create the life that you hold dear
You want to grow, it's in your heart
Now all you have to do is start
But what is it that holds you back
Diverts your focus to sidetrack?
So what, your ducks aren't in a row!
And yes, there's more that you don't know
So even if it starts real slow
The secret is you must just go!

If you insist on full perfection
You bind your time with introspection
Overwhelmed with its complexion
Exploring every intersection
Fearful of assured rejection
Diverting you from your direction
Requiring further self-inspection
Uncovering every single imperfection
This time a thorough retrospection
And all that's done is circumspection

Get off the curb, you need some action
And not the kind found in abstraction
You have a plan, you know what to do
The truth is, nothing's stopping you
Let fears or worries of what may come
Be just one more thing you've overcome
Hold tight the vision of what could be
As you build your new reality
Forget the past and what has been
Jump with both feet, and just begin!

HEAVENLY
THOUGHTS

Section 2: Heavenly Thoughts

If my journey to explore and learn about happiness has taught me anything, it is that a connection to our Source, the Divine Creator, a Force or a Cause bigger than we are, is imperative!

The way we pray or meditate, who we worship, the frequency, the format is not nearly as important as the connection itself. Knowing there was something or someone before us who will be there long after we are gone helps to put our own lives in perspective.

Eckhart Tolle, in his book *A New Earth*, describes an image of the soul as illuminated silhouette to our ego. Our human incarnation with all its flaws and need to be right needs to be acknowledged, and emotional messiness seen as a dark shadow standing in front of the lighted soul.

When you work to see only the potential, the Child of God in the Soul, and ignore the shadow of the ego as much as possible... the results are amazing!

And so, a few poems on these
Heavenly Thoughts... Enjoy!

~ The Queen of Happiness

ARMY OF ANGELS

The news is bad, as evil lurks,
    the world is filled with crooks and jerks
      we hear about them all day long
        the news, the movies and the songs

It seems as if they truly strive
    to make it real, control our lives
      and all that we can do is watch
        the horror of their stale *death*watch

And as we take it all inside,
    assume the worst of all implied,
      that's when we really take it in,
        become suspicious and begin

To think the worst of those we see
    in fact, we think that all must be
      a danger or at the very least
        a raging and uncaring beast

And this is what we start to find
    since firmly planted in our mind
      are thoughts of crooks and jerks and more
        We start to judge and act before

We stop to think or wonder why
    these awful thoughts unleashed to fly.
      But here is what you need to know
        (It comes from ancient wisdoms, yo!)

What you think is who you'll be
   and what you look for is what you'll see!

Unfiltered input tends to lean
   toward the rude and toward the mean
      It's easy to allow that poo
         to build up high inside of you

But just like anything you own,
   what is reaped is what is sown
      Ignore your garden, you get weeds
         but tend it well and you get seeds

And so it is your mind's the same -
   what you plant is what you gain
      Guard your spirit from dark despair
         It's up to you to fill the air

With love and joy and happy news
   The beauty is you get to choose
      what goes in and what you keep
         and what you send to the trash heap

Turn off the news and grab your shoes
   and start to make each day infused
      with happy thoughts and smiles for all
         Throwback your head and stand up tall

To show the world though evil lurks
   that though there are still crooks and jerks
      that most of us are really nice
         that smiling *first* means smiling twice

The world is full of helpful folks
   who want the best and work for strokes
      A smile and thanks can go all the way
         to turn around someone's bad day

So I am sure that we can prove
   with one giant and collective move
      we can ignore the dreary unhappy news,
         move the mountains, erase the blues

Go out and use *The Force* for good
   Let no one question where we stood
      to turn the tide to show the rest
         that we don't have to pass their test

That there's always another way
   one filled with hope and love. We pray
      for strength and courage as well as grace
         and wear our blessings on our face.

So tune out those harmful ugly ways
   to bring about just joy-filled days
      It's up to you and one another
         each one we meet, sister or brother

And so you warriors use what you know
   Go out each day and make it so!
      Assume the best! Ignore the rest!
         And when you find yourself distressed....

Just stop and breathe in all God's grace
   Remember as you run the race:
      The rats will win if you sit by
         Your silence won't bestill the lie

Since all it takes
   to make love true
      is an Army of Angels
         disguised as you!

WARRIOR SPIRIT

Warrior Spirit, come inside!
Fill me up with strength and pride
Let courage flow, let glad heart sing
Let words and deeds and thoughts all bring
Warrior Angels to stand with me
Divine strength flows and now I'm free
Shoulders squared, though fear abounds
Head held high, though all around
Uncertainty and doubt and pain
Come driving down like sheets of rain
To soak me in its cold wet plight
To try to drown out Spirit's Light
But with Angel Guards protecting me
And Spirit's Light inside of me
I know whatever must be faced
Can now be met – with strength and grace

ON GUARDIAN ANGELS

Though seldom seen and rarer heard
Consigned before our birth occurred
Concealed within our inner core
As guide to Spirit, poised to soar
Revealed through heart, not head nor thought
Conspires through dreams as lessons taught
Connecting soul to higher strength
Prepared to wait whate'er the length
Prompting acts inspired by right
To gladden toward the ray of light
Till wisdom's grace provides the gift
Once known, then recognition swift
Beauty revealed in mercies learned
Forgiveness grows, intent discerned
A lifelong friend, bonds intertwined
Awaits the call that Joy assigned
To guard the soul from ego's greed
Shine light on Spirit's cherished need
To guide from innocence to knowledge then
Provide the light to wisdoms glen
Encouraging life as dark descends
With us long past this journey ends

SOUL LIGHT

Within each of us resides a light
A spark conceived of Love made real
Reflecting what in grace's sight
The world conspires to soon conceal

Born with clear, unclouded view
Soon earthly knowing shields the beam
And truths that once we surely knew
Turn forgotten shimmers in the stream

The ego's call for puff and pride,
Assumes a stance of supervision
Guiding choices in its stride
Creating states of indecision

Led by needs of expectations
Justice, fairness, righteousness
Grown to look for explanations
Validation's sightlessness

Shadows fall across the ray
When settling for the moments lure
Seeking self simply delays
The quiet joy of soul's demure

The ego's coffers never fill,
As want defines a haunting chase
But Soul Light seeks only to thrill
And guide us on our road to Grace

The course each soul must long traverse,
Is, by design, a competition
Mind and spirit ofttimes adverse
With little common disposition

The Spark, reflecting love alone,
Asks naught but be allowed to shine
And aches to give you all you own
If it's the rod you'd so divine

Peace, compassion, ease of heart,
Forgiveness, joy, and radiance
Restore the soul as fears depart
Replaced by blessings ever hence

Abandoned, ego's cravings pale
To trust in Love's unfolding force
As gratitude assumes the veil
Of humbleness before the Source

And so each choice, each act, each breath must choose
To reflect the light Spirit bestows
Or meekly pay the ego's dues
Denying debts which grace exposed

Have faith surrender reaps rewards
Far greater than when ego's needs are sought,
It's all you need to move towards
The Light and Source of all that's taught

THOUGHTS ON A PLANE

From azure to cerulean blue
The clouds become a tundra's view
All thoughts for this moment, quite objective
Observed from this unique perspective
Daily details fill morn till night
Conclude with sleep's exhausted flight
No time to think, much less reflect
A moment's daydream feels suspect
Just rush from work to home to bed
But right now, finds me here instead
With hours stretching, quite unable
To continue working life's timetable
Forced to enjoy the spectacular view
Moments like this so rare and few
Alone with thoughts that continue unheeded
Solitude, at times, is needed
To get to know one's self again
Re-acquaint the heart, like an old friend
Remembering passions of long ago
Ideals replaced with a life on the go
Retrieving pieces of what once was me
One who took the time to see
All revealed in moments such
When cloud and sky revealed God's Touch

LIFE IS HARD!

Section 3: Life is Hard

It is simply unrealistic to expect every moment in life to be happy. That would simply be setting ourselves up for disappointment. In fact, it's not all that hard to be happy when life is going your way. In fact, it is when life is not going our way that we need a little help.

First, have acceptance that trouble will appear, that's *when* not *if*. Then, have an understanding that while we enjoy the easy times, we learn from and grow from the troubled ones. Everyone you meet is a teacher, teaching you who you want to be or who you do not.

I believe wholeheartedly that as we grow in gratitude and tolerance, we grow in happiness and acceptance, of our lives, our roles, our duty. Happiness is not about having an easy life. Hardly anyone gets to run away and join the circus (insert your happiness fantasy here).

The following poems were all written for those times, those days, those moments when happiness seems elusive and trouble a constant companion that you cannot seem to hide from.

So, knowing Life is Hard,
Enjoy!

The Queen of Happiness

OH YEAH, SISTER,
LIFE CAN BE HARD

Oh yeah, Sister, life can be hard
Sometimes you can't even see the reward
It feels like the whole world is leaning on you
Asking for help with their problems anew
And being the strong one, holding together
The turmoil accompanying such stormy weather

You know that they need you to be strong for their sake
Accepting the load, you so willingly take
Your courage and competence relied on each day
None of them realizing the price that you pay
And you want to be there, helping with all
The troubles and struggles your loved ones befall

But there comes a time when, despite your intentions
To be there for all of their strife and rejections
You are the one who needs special care
Your back cannot handle the burdens you bear
And just for a time you must take care of you
Regaining your strength so that Spirit can renew

You'll be good to no one if your energy's tapped
Your resources used and enthusiasm capped
It's time that you take out some time to relax
And regain the strength and the essence you've taxed
For even a geyser is dormant at times
Gathering strength for the next time it climbs

And just don't you worry about those you would help
It's time that they learned to rely on themselves
You've shown them the way and then taught them besides
The strength and the courage that they have inside
Your stepping aside will provide them the chance
To begin to handle their own circumstance

So rest and recharge, you'll be called on again
The need for your guidance, that never will end
But right now the one who needs help most from you
Is the face in the mirror, who deserves your love too!
So play and enjoy, delight, rest and learn
You're worth it sister, and right now, it's your turn!

IT'S NOT ABOUT ME

It isn't really all that hard
To have your feelings hurt
When you stop to scrutinize
Each and every word we blurt
Convinced that all you hear and knew
Is actually and only all about you
When life is hard and that's all you can see,
Just say to yourself,
"It's Not About Me!"

Rude behavior, cutting in line,
Moving too slowly and taking their time
Traffic rage at thoughtless drivers
Is it you making them your pain revivers?
But you can have freedom if you can see
The pain is theirs,
"It's Not About Me!"

Thoughtless comments pierce your heart
Angry outbursts play their part
As disappointment when you're not heard
Begins a hurt that you've transferred
It's easy to take it all personally
The secret to remember is,
"It's Not About Me!"

When fear is near we all lash out
At anyone who's close
And closeness, sadly, specifies
Just who we hurt the most
But it's been said, just because it's said
Does not mean that it is true
And the thoughtless, hurtful actions are about
The sender and not you
Not everyone is mindful of
The person they might be
But you don't have to take it in if you know,
"It's Not About Me!"

"If you can keep your head when all about you
Are losing theirs and blaming it on you"
Begin the words that help describe
What we all aspire to accrue
To maintain Grace with head held high
When no Grace to you is offered
To shine your light for all to see
When you easily could have suffered
To make the world a better place,
Offer forgiveness abundantly
It's easy to do and it's all up to you to live as if
"It's Not About Me!"

Note: "If you can keep your head when all about you
Are losing theirs and blaming it on you"
IF by Rudyard Kipling

IT SEEMS TROUBLE
FOLLOWS YOU AROUND

It seems trouble follows you around
   Then brings life crashing round your ears
Indeed, although, you'd not be found
   It found you first, in all your fears

A breath is taken, deeply seized
   Resolute in facing all you must
Refusing quarter, refuse to please
   Turning now to One you trust

With faith in Spirit to sustain
   Through whatever path you tread
Assured the future carries pain
   But draw the strength to move ahead

You yield to plans you'd naught selected
   Determined to look for lessons taught
And find the joy when unexpected
   Glimpsing moments never to be bought

More precious every day does grow
   As worries from a time now gone
Pale against what now you know
   Forget conclusions once forgone

Each day's challenge soon is found
   From success so bravely wrought
Some days courage all abounds
   Some, there's none, though gamely sought
Through tears and anger a voice is heard
   To sing the song your life proclaims
The comfort flows form every word
   No need to give the truth a name
You know a peace, a deep respect
   Forgiveness living in your face
Your beauty shines and then reflects
   Bathed in the light of Spirit's Grace

NAUGHT THE LESSON

When things are good, and times are high
We seldom stop to question why
Or take the chance to jeopardize
The sweet release that bliss supplies
No questions asked or analyzed
As current pleasures tantalized
Forgotten in felicity
And joys found in simplicity
To bask in moments purely grand
Oblige no urge to understand

And though as much as any soul
I love the moment's happiness
I also know at times we stroll
Along the anguish of distress
When days are dark, and all is lost
We're forced to face what most we fear
Of what we have and what it cost
And to which values we adhere

As patience, strength and faith are tested
Future wisdoms all are vested
Lessons learned, we grow beyond
Expand our lives and break the bond
Of chains we make of limitations
Rejecting all their implications
Unaware that tribulations
Often lead to inspirations
Pain and suffering rarely seen
As, naught the lesson, but the mean

So revel when the glory days
Bring joy and sunshine across your course
Diminish not the happy ways
You join in union with your Source
But in times when hope seems far away
When grace and courage are required
Take heart that what you give today
Is not half as much as you've acquired

ELUSIVE DREAMS

As daylight fades to early eve
We walk toward twilight, journey's end
Navigating as we go
The rough and bumps to round the bend
No time to waste or gather wool,
Each moment counts, and they are few
The lists of tasks run through your mind
Long after work and day are through

You've changed your clothes and washed your face
Now nestled in amongst the down
Still thinking of your chores and deeds
Your minds awhirl, your brow a frown
You watch the clock as darkness drags out
Sounds from deep within the night
Each creak or groan begets a glance
That only validates your plight

You do the math and count the hours
Of sleep you will not soon win back
You tell yourself you'll clear your mind,
And try another failed tack
As thoughts begin to wander far
Beyond the reach of sunshine's beam
Suggestions of a dark night's ghost
Soon become all that they may seem

Elusive dreams look far away
No matter how eagerly or earnestly sought
How does the state you long to find
Become the very one you've fought?
For what awaits the dreamer when
His conscience thoughts no longer shield
The soul from contact with these strange
Alluring plans we fly afield?

Without wakeful inhibitions
We are freed to move beyond
The mortal bonds and boundaries to which
Form and logic correspond
With conscience thought suspended
All the thresholds open wide
Worlds and ideas unimagined
Beckon us to come inside

Swirls of color set the stage
For creatures never seen before
Characters and situations
Presented so to be explored
Inhibitions absent let us
Dance within our sleep
Imagery and symbolism reveal
Secrets buried deep

Surrendering one's fear is required
To revel in dreaming spirit's flight
To leave oneself exposed to views
Of terror and then delight
Letting go of daytime thoughts
And all conclusions that we hold
Releases truths to be disclosed
As bold revealing dreams unfold

As you embrace uncovered secrets
Embracing a crisp new world view
Empowered by the knowledge gained
Of all you already knew
Throwing off the fear of nighttime's
cloaking, cloying, clinging clutch
Relinquishing the boundaries
That limit consciousness's touch

And look forward to surrender
To a nature not of this plane
Knowing you may find a view
Your current world cannot contain
And heed the lessons seeping in from thoughts
You didn't know you dreamed
As each day's foils and let downs then
Can each night be redeemed

No longer lying dreading every
Inching moment to no avail
Now eager to lay me down each night
To sail on spirits astral trail
Grow to welcome all adventures
And accept soaring wings
Embracing blissful, restful, soulful
Sleep and all it brings.

GIVING GRACE

Section 4: Giving Grace

Grace is defined as unearned mercy or love in our lives. We look for and find the grace—in the times we have been forgiven, the times when our mistakes have been overlooked, when we received love but felt like we didn't deserve it.

Every day we are afforded opportunities to Give Grace to ourselves, to our loved ones, and to the world around us. Each time we smile first, forgive easily, or comfort without thoughts to our own needs we are paying forward or simply sharing all the grace our lives already hold. Like any skill, Giving Grace simply requires a commitment, practice and follow through. But the benefits are life changing.

And so it begins. You notice the peace (grace) in which you are living ...people are nicer, life is easier, and conflict and negativity begin to not so much disappear as become far less important. This is living in the state of grace.

Start by counting the blessings in your life, one by one, day by day, every day. Remember and acknowledge all the forgiveness and grace that has been shown to you. Keep a gratitude journal close to you. Physically write down (and read later) all the blessings in your life at least once a day.

Next, approach every relationship, every interpersonal interaction as if you were meeting a Divine Soul, the purest self, the self of all potential, no matter how their ego may be treating you right then. Forgive everyone that you can. Forgive yourself if you are still working on it.

And third, love yourself. Learning to love yourself, all of you, all parts of you, the good the bad and the ugly, is what grows in you the grace, the ability, to pay that forward. As you see the grace that has been afforded you, you create a space in your life for generosity, resulting in grace in someone else's life.

Learn to forgive yourself. See your own soul in the group of Divinity you honor in everyone and everything around you, and see what that does for your level of everyday happiness.

I hope you see all the ways you are Giving Grace every day…. Enjoy! TQOH

CARE FOR EACH OTHER

Our birth was a promise to be fulfilled
Becoming the foundation
The warm embrace and sheltered space
Was love's own confirmation
From child to adult naive we grew,
Sacrifice unsuspected
Unconscious of both deeds and words
That nourished and protected

For as we grew, the care received
Came at a certain cost
Of time and talent forfeited
And sleep and all that's lost
Then as we gain in years and climb
And so earn a new perspective
It's then we see that getting sleep
Was never the objective

As those that nursed and formed our youth
Are nearing journey's end
In honoring our place in life,
The cycle starts again
As those who had been tended for,
Now become those who would tend
The process now transcending roles,
Allows love to so contend

Honor wisdom gained from hours on earth,
To laugh, to cry, to just survive
We all fight this fight, to learn to thrive,
From the moment we arrive
Then as we return God's precious gift,
Received when we began
Fulfilled as we tenderly care for each other,
Over and over again

YEARS FROM NOW

Years from now, when time's flown by
And the passage of years is the blink of an eye
When life's tribulations and troubles all seem
Like some foggy memory of a long-faded dream

When heartache and frustration vex us no longer
And what didn't kill us indeed made us stronger
When triumph and regret take their place in the scheme
And we've climbed every mountain, forded each stream

We'll look back across the oh so many years
Lives filled with laughter, fears, beers and tears
And know whatever life threw us, be it big or it small
We faced it together, friends through it all.

CELEBRATE! REMEMBER!

We're born alone and die alone,
But in between we're shown
How our lives are touched and shaped and warmed
By each one that we've known
But there are some who touch our soul
So deeply that they stay
Forever with us in our hearts,
Even when they've gone away

As these are souls who bring to life
The means of joy's design
And squeeze the most from every hour,
Even as those hours decline
Their lives a celebration
Of their journey traveled well
A light shining on the lucky ones
Upon whom they've cast their spell

A presence thereon whom we call
To share what needs be known
And bask in the encouragement
That would assuredly be shown
Connected souls live in our core,
Connected in our hearts
An endless influence guiding us
With wisdom to impart

The battle for a life is known
In every breath that's drawn
For each of us will end some day
And that is long foregone
To resist enduring forces conspiring
To capture our delight
Is the gift that we aspire to and hope
to bring into the fight

As we race along the journey that
We each are meant to tread
As supporter or survivor
Or in place of one instead
Who, in spite of valiant effort,
Left the race oh far too soon
We will Celebrate! Remember!
And Fight Back! Under the moon

We honor those who forged such lives
For their triumph is complete
In a way they lift our souls with lives
Of joy and lives replete
With a legacy long lasting
From those who exist to shine a light
That the secret to a life well lived
Is to learn to love the fight!

GIVING GRACE

You look around your blessed days
Abundance bounds beyond mere means
You're working hard and well it pays
And life is good and so it seems

A debt is owed the world at large
In gratitude for this largesse
To turn your back ignores the charge
Denying grace's gratefulness

To acknowledge gifts concedes the dues
That gratitude begins to pay
To some there's still much more to do
And those are you addressed today

Your gift of vigor, time and force
In exchange for life so richly blessed
Assumed that duty is the source
Required of you, and never guessed

That you are Spirit's reflecting light
The touch of angels on your face
The debt you pay becomes delight
As blessed you are with Giving Grace

CHOICES

Our lives are a series of choices we make
A product of the paths we take
Each day a fresh start from beginning to end
A chance each time to begin again
We create the person we want to be
Our actions are our legacy

The manner that we choose each day
Defines our lives along the way
To offer kindness unexpected
Assistance though it's not requested
Deciding if you'll give all you've got to give
Determines the life you elect to live

The days then weeks then months then years
Grow into a lifetime and soon it appears
You've written the story that now bears your name
The sum of your days and your choices became
A book wide open for the whole world to see
Make sure it's the tale that you want it to be

Versology (or musings on these verses)

HAPPINESS

THE QUEEN OF HAPPINESS

The Queen of Happiness changed the trajectory of my life. After a random comment made a significant impact, I wrote this poem and then adopted The Queen's persona as my alter ego. Today I work hard to embody The Queen of Happiness both professionally and in my everyday life.

SMILE! SMILE! SMILE!

Long ago, I learned that the single biggest weapon available in our happiness arsenal is our smile and I try to wield mine daily. It's easy, it's available, it's free and it's contagious! Science agrees that the act of smiling, even when it is a manual response, boosts our endorphins, changes the way we see things, and changes the way people respond to us.

Once you start putting out the smile (to everyone you meet, at work, in the car, in the mirror) you might notice your mood elevating, your thoughts becoming more positive, people becoming nicer to you.

After offering this advice for years, here it is in the form of verse.

It's not a gimmick! Give it a try!

A KINDNESS DEFICIT

The Kindness Deficit came from my adamant belief that in every moment (in every thought) we have the chance to choose. Every moment is the option to lift-up or tear down, ourselves and those around us.

That's right, we get to choose our thoughts, our words, our deeds. You might notice a continued theme that the sum of these choices determines our happiness. But just what is happiness?

HAPPINESS

Eckhart Tolle, author of *A New Earth*, offered a definition of happiness that has had an immense impact on me. He says happiness comes in 3 levels:
-   Ecstasy,
-   Enjoyment, and
-   Acceptance.

I suppose I have taken this idea and run with it, plus added a few thoughts of my own.

Ecstasy is sometimes described as the state of flow. Vibrating at our highest levels we are living in love and acceptance and are in line with our purpose, our passion, our Creator. We know these moments when they happen. The sky is a little bluer, the wind has a whisper of the wisdom of the ages. In this state, time seems to stand still. We might find this state through prayer or meditation, extreme exercise or dance, creating art, while staring at a sleeping baby, having sex, sitting on a mountaintop. No one argues with Ecstasy.

Next, *Enjoyment*, where we probably spend most of our time. Dinner with the kids, laughing and joking. Driving to work, planning our day, hot water in the morning shower, leisure activities, entertainment, consumption. We are alive, we are smiling, we are busy, we are happy. This is where we live.

Finally, *Acceptance*, because life is not always a bowl of cherries and there are moments we do not love. Conflict with our loved ones, disappointments, bad decisions, loss, challenges and tears are all apart of all our lives. To pretend differently is simply dishonest. Accepting those moments, allowing ourselves to feel unhappy emotions rather than run from them or suppress them is a part of being happy.

When you count your blessings, when you love and are loved, you create the space to sit with less than fun emotions until they have served their purpose, brought the lessons, shined the light. Acceptance of life's unexpected direction and challenges, living inside the moment and not hiding from them, takes away all the power of these emotions.

JUST BEGIN

I don't know about you, but I am a world class procrastinator. I want to have it all perfect, all thought through. And yet, what I have learned is that instead, you just must just suck it up and get it done. Success rewards actions and there are no substitutes.

Now I am not knocking planning or making lists or doing research or getting feedback or starting over or all of the other things we do to avoid taking the plunge or take a risk. Life is a series of new beginnings and the more we put them off, the more new beginnings we might be missing.

HEAVENLY THOUGHTS

ARMY OF ANGELS

I have always wanted to write a rap, admiring the pace and the complex rhymes, it seemed right up my alley. One day, I sat down, and a stream of rhymes seemed to be calling me from the aether. I could barely type fast enough to keep up with each thought as they appeared. About 45 minutes later, I slumped back, exhausted. "Oh my gosh," I thought, "I think I just wrote a rap!"

This all came about a few months after I myself had "turned off the news." A former news and media junkie, I finally realized the constant barrage of horrible news just did not correspond to my reality. My experience most days was filled with positive interactions with caring people actively engaged in making a better life for themselves, their families, and the world around them

The information about things that did not directly impact me about people I did not know was not offering anything positive to my life. When I turned off the news, I started paying more attention to the people I do know and see every day. Now I am an avid reader of our local small-town newspaper and follow City Council decisions. That is news enough for me.

This poem has become the mantra for my life

WARRIOR SPIRIT

I believe Angels are around us. They come to comfort, teach or bolster us and, sometimes, they are there to stand beside and fight for us. During a difficult time, a time that I was not sure I had the strength to do what was required, it was this warrior spirit that held me up.

Printing this verse on the graphic of a strong warrior angel and putting it in the front of my folder, I read it over again. Knowing I was not alone, that angels stood beside me helped me to hold up my head, speak strongly and proudly knowing I was loved and protected.

ON GUARDIAN ANGELS

More than just one of the Angels around us, our guardian angels are more personal, sent to watch over us. They mean to have a personal relationship with us, if we let them. Our cheerleader for the soul, this special envoy is here with us every day, giving love, giving light, giving guidance. Embrace your guardian angel!

SOUL LIGHT

Inside each of us is a constant battle between our true selves, our infinite and divine selves and the ego, our personality or earthly human side. We are born in this Divine Light, but soon the egos of the earthly selves around us "teach" us of the ways of the world.

We spend our entire lives on the epic journey to return to the Joy and Perfection found in our (re)union with our Divine Spark. Whether we realize it or not, this battle is waging in every choice we make, in every thought we have. From the ego's view, we argue, need to be right, need to be acknowledged and validated.

When we approach life from the Soul's perspective, we learn to relinquish control, see the Divine in everyone and everything we meet, live from a place of gratitude and service. And as we awaken to this constant battle, we begin to act, not react. We begin to consciously choose and direct our energy.

Feed your soul...the payoff is Bliss....

THOUGHTS ON A PLANE

The life of a working mom, devoted activist and regular volunteer, did not leave much time for thoughts about soul vs ego, forgiveness, grace etc. These were far removed from my then daily life.

Stuck on a business flight with no electronics, no books and nothing to do for several hours but look out the window and reflect, I realized how little of my time was devoted to devotion, to self-care, to my own happiness in general. I saw the whirling dervish I had become and realized that moments watching my children sleep, enjoying a warm bath or lost in prayer were few and far between.

I won't say I stepped off the plane and changed my life, but it all begins with a slight shift in perspective. Looking back, though I did not realize it at the time, this moment was indeed, a significant shift.

LIFE IS HARD

OH, YEAH, SISTER, LIFE CAN BE HARD

Years ago, my sister-in-law, Sandy (one of my angels in heaven now), was going through a hard time in her life. She was so accustomed to taking care of all around her and was worried about them as she was forced to put the focus on herself.

This poem was an encouragement to her that *she* was one of the people who needed her care. In fact, she needed it the most. It seems this happens often for many women, especially those who are natural care givers.

IT'S NOT ABOUT ME

My life got so much simpler when I realized that 90% of all that I worry and stew about is simply not about me. It seems we project our fears and concerns onto the world around us.

When we assume "it's all about me," it's easy to be off to the races with worry, anger, or resentment. Almost everyone is so busy fighting their own battles, their troubles or rudeness or lack of concern or whatever speaks to what they are going through. This does not have to include you if you don't allow it.

IT SEEMS TROUBLE FOLLOWS YOU AROUND

Written for a friend dealing with a difficult medical prognosis, this poem speaks to the gifts and grace of tragedy and hardship. You hear the tale repeatedly of those grateful for a near fatal diagnosis or incident, grateful for the shift, for the perspective of gratitude for daily existence, a realization of priorities, and any misalignment with daily actions.

May we each appreciate these things with or without a life changing experience. May we stop to find the grace in our troubles, the beauty in our suffering, and the gifts these times reveal.

NAUGHT THE LESSON

Again, sticking with the theme of Life is Hard, it occurs to me, even on a search for happiness, that we simply cannot be happy at every moment. Struggle and challenge have always been and always will be a part of every life. It's hard to see the bigger picture when we are in the middle of the lesson, but the one thought we can hold onto is that growth can come from pain.

While we love the celebration, the post-accomplishment high, the satisfaction of a job well done or time well spent, those are the payoffs for work, anguish, pain and effort. Lessons come from climbing over our mistakes. Enjoy the good for sure, but know the growth is even in the pain.

ELUSIVE DREAMS

Honestly, this is one of my favorite pieces in this collection. With so many words (in every sentence!) it can be a bit thick and laborious to read through. I've started to change it a thousand times, but the truth is, this is exactly what I wanted to say.

If you find this verse difficult to follow, the recording may   help.

www.thequeenofhappiness.com/elusivedreams. With its long and winding sentences, it may require a little direction or inflection to best appreciate and listening through may help.

Embracing the night, looking forward to sleep, and having the confidence that sleep will come swiftly and deeply is simply the same as working through anything we may want to manifest. What we hold in our thoughts and feel in our hearts is what is made real in our lives.

Don't run from the respite we are each given each night, to fly the astral plane and to reset our psyche. Plunge in, as if diving under the waves and just float to your true alternate reality.

GIVING GRACE

CARE FOR EACH OTHER

It became clear through a series of events that my aging parents, alone in the Midwest, could no longer take care of their large house and perhaps even themselves, and we began the process to move them across the country to the West Coast and in with us.

As I processed this unexpected life change, searching for ways to make it okay, I had a vision I can only describe as a waking dream. Sitting in the garden, deep in thought, I saw the full cycle of parents caring for children, enriching their grandchildren, being tended to as children by their children. It was so beautiful, so just. It felt exactly the way it is supposed to be. It was another giant shift in perspective that led me to see and know the honor of caring for those who cared for me.

YEARS FROM NOW

Good friends are those that know us best, are with us at the best and worst moments, and share the memories that are sometimes not fit to share with others. Thinking about how current moments would translate to future memories, I wrote this short poem to honor the place friendship holds in our hearts. (It makes a great gift or card!).

Friends are the family we choose.

CELEBRATE! REMEMBER!

A young friend asked me to write a poem honoring his grandmother. She was a larger than life hero to the entire family and her early departure was still being grieved, 10 years after she had gone.

We all have someone in our lives who reinforces the adage "only the good die young." This poem honors someone specific in one set of lives, but perhaps speaks for all of our heroes who are taken too soon.

GIVING GRACE

Grace: defined as mercy or unearned love, love undeserved. We all have had need of it, and we all are given numerous opportunities to offer it. I just can't help but think that Grace and the giving of Grace is inextricably linked to happiness.

In Grace, we offer love to those who may have not offered love at all. Grace requires forgiveness. My own strategy is to recall when Grace was shown to me. This makes me grateful and full of love and offers the generosity to "pay it forward." Does this take effort? Yes! But the payoff is a light heart, a clear mind, and karma in the bank!

CHOICES

This poem, written over 20 years ago, has been for years my signature go-to verse. It encapsulates the theme I hope you are feeling throughout this book— that is, that happiness is a choice, that every choice we make leads us to happiness (or not) and that understanding why we are making the choices we do and what their impacts will be is, indeed, the single biggest factor in determining (at least, my own) happiness.

When we slow down, forgive everyone, take care of ourselves physically and spiritually, when we address the Divine in everyone we see, and see only the soul's potential in others versus the ego we have to deal with, we begin to make choices that lead to an honest and lasting happiness. Adopting love, gratitude, forgiveness, kindness, and an indifference to outcomes can make for a shaman-like blissful existence that is available to anyone, regardless of circumstances.

About the Author

Tina Ann has been writing and performing her poetry in public for almost 30 years. She draws on her experiences as a mother, grandmother, corporate professional, speaker, actress, comedienne, and general free spirit to create poetry that not only has messages for everyday life but is easy and fun to read.

Tina Ann offers a unique combination of creativity and analytics. She finds herself enamored not only with the rhyming verse but also the process of creating that verse, the same way she views happiness and the process of achieving it. She has used this talent to create unique personal gifts, tributes and positive statements on life.

In this, her first published collection of poetry, Tina Ann uses her talents for painting pictures with words and storytelling to share ideas and perspective for a happier life and her analytic nature to break down how to achieve this.

Tina Ann shares a beautiful house by the beach with the man of her dreams and two adorable dogs, and shares her life with a combined family that includes 7 children, 13 grandchildren, mom, sons-in-law and granddogs, extended family, and friends.

Working hard to balance a beautiful life at home with the excitement of regular performances and appearances, Tin Ann is a Speaker, Comedienne, Author, Actress, and now, Published Poet!

Acknowledgements

I have no words to describe the feelings of elation and accomplishment (and I'm a poet!) I am feeling as I complete this project. None of it would have been possible without all of you and a few folks I would like to mention specifically

My man, Richard (Dickfish), who is indeed my biggest fan, even if he doesn't really like poetry. But he does like me, loves me, and does whatever it takes to help me to tackle and achieve my dreams ...even when they take me far from him. There is simply no substitute for being loved unconditionally by someone who does not have to (out of a familial obligation) love you. It offers you the total freedom to be who you are and, for me, has been the single biggest factor in my journey, to become who I am today. For all of this, and so much more, I am forever grateful.

My children, the Fab 5, the Wild Bunch, my biggest accomplishments...they have laughed with me, cried with me, and supported me like a parent might a precocious child. I hope that while they were rolling their eyes and making Boomer jokes at my expense, they learned to pursue every one of their dreams, when no one shares that dream with them. This is the only legacy that truly matters.

My parents, who told me they loved me every day and made me truly believe I could go anywhere I wanted to go, do anything I wanted to do, and be anyone I wanted to be (as long as I was home by 10:30 ☺). They gave me and my siblings a quiet Midwest suburban life, unmarred by any sort of intrigue, excitement or danger, and yet, the life that movies are made of...fun, drama, romance, theatre roles, drive-ins and skating rinks. My little world played out so uneventfully on my very small stage……maybe my first little glimpse of heaven.

My dear friend, Arjan Lin, kindred souls who met and instantly connected, supporting each other through triumph and tragedy. Everyone needs someone in their life who keeps them grounded, keeps them connected, calls for no reason but to see how you are, picks up conversations where the last one left off a month later as if no time had passed, able to look you in the eye and tell you what you need to hear, not what you want to hear kind of friend. I am so lucky to have one.

My dear friend, Vivian, another kindred soul with whom the connection was so strong, that we remain friends 20 years later after a very brief stint as coworkers. Our love has crossed the heartaches and the miles of a long-distance friendship that is, to this day, one of the most cherished relationships in my life. Her input, her humor (her gifs), her encouragement and belief in me helped make this book possible.

My assistant, Jordan, who made sure I was on task, moving forward and focused on today's objectives, not the freight train of grand ambitions I become when excited about an idea. Jordan makes the standstills start moving, the impossible seem trivial and the forgotten visible. Every artist needs someone to help make the vision become real and, for me, that someone is Jordan.

To my friends, all of you, who continue to support my many incarnations, characters, adventures and challenges, no matter how crazy….(and all of which seem to end up with my being on the stage or in front of the camera): thank you for finding me funny (seriously), inspirational, or at least entertaining while enduring my ADHD time/date issues.

And finally, well, everyone! Neighbors, party attendees, acquaintances, colleagues, fellow volunteers, co-workers, and random strangers who happened to be within earshot of my sharing a poem, a thought or a song, have all contributed to this moment. Thank you to all who have encouraged me over the years, clapped at my impromptu performances, complimented my writing, liked and commented on my posts.

I hope you enjoy this first collection of my poems.

Tina Ann, TQOH

More from Tina Ann

There was a girl who liked to rhyme
Every day and all the time
Every word she ever uttered
Whispered, shouted, spewed or stuttered
Came out sounding like another
Word she'd said before the other

Her family liked it fine at first
This tendency to speak in verse
They showed her off, they told their friends
Perhaps she'd start some brand-new trends
They thought her way of endless versing
Could be worse – she could be cursing!

But soon the rhymes began to wear
Her family, though, to be quite fair,
Endured her rhyming, singsong ways
Convinced that it would end some day
But years went by, and up she grew
Still rhyming all she liked to do

It has been suggested that Tina Ann's next book, *There Was a Girl Who Liked to Rhyme and Other Tales That Might be True* is, perhaps, a bit autobiographical. In any case it is the delightful tale of a girl with a talent and a message. In this collection of stories in verse, we are invited into worlds we didn't dream we didn't know of.

There Was a Girl is available for pre-order. The expected publication Summer 2020. Register for my fan list to ensure your copy today! www.thequeenofhappiness.com